Scriptural Commands for Modern Times Living God's Word TodayVolume3

Joshua Rhoades

Published by Joshua Paul Rhoades, 2024.

SCRIPTURAL COMMANDS FOR MODERN TIMES LIVING GOD'S WORD TODAYVOLUME3

First edition. September 5, 2024.

Copyright © 2024 Joshua Rhoades.

ISBN: 979-8227441669

Written by Joshua Rhoades.

Also by Joshua Rhoades

Courage Under Fire: David's Stand On The Battlefield

Jonah's Journey: Voices Of Redemption And Lessons In Obedience

The Furnace Of Faith: 12 Principles From The Heat Of Faith

Whispers of Hope: Inspiring Stories of Men's Prayers In Scripture

Frontier Legends: The Oregon Dream

Elijah: A Beacon Of Boldness

HOOK, LINE & SAVIOUR - Faith Reflections from Fishing

Driven By Faith: Motor Racing Inspired Christian Life

30 Day Devotional - Bold and Strong- Coffee Devotions for a Courageous Christian Walk

Authentic Christianity: The Heart of Old Time Religion

Consider The Ant - God's Tiny Preachers

Flee Fornication: The Plea For Purity

Renewed Hope- How to Find Encouragement in God

Sounding The Call - The Voice of Conviction

The Altar - Where Heaven Meets Earth

The Bible's Battlefields- Timeless Lessons from Ancient Wars

The Sacred Art of Silence - How Silence Speaks in Scripture

Under Fire- The Sanctity of the Traditional Biblical Home

Who Is on the Lord's Side? A Call to Righteousness

What Is Truth? - From Skepticism to Submission

First and Goal- Faith and Football Fundamentals

From Dugout to Devotion- Spiritual Lessons from Baseball

Par for the Course- Faith and Fairways

The Believer's Pace- Tools for Running Life's Marathon

The Immutable Fortress- Security in God's Unchanging Nature
Biblical Bravery
Deer Stands and Devotions: A Hunter's Walk with God
Jesus Knows- Our Hearts, Our Responsibility
Restoration - Setting The Bone
Spiritual 911- God's Word for Life's Emergency's
The Freedom of Forgiveness
The Jezebel Effect - Ancient Manipulations Modern Lessons
The Shout That Stopped The Saviour
The Time Machine Chronicles: Old Testament Characters
Anchored In Truth Exploring The Depths of Psalm 119
Biblical Counsel on Anger
Proverbs' Portraits The Men God Mentions
Stumbling in the Dark - The Dangers of Alcohol
Guarding the Wicket Protecting Your Faith and Game
The Champion's Faith - Wrestling and Achieving Spiritual Victory
Scriptural Commands for Modern Times Living God's Word Today
Volume 1
Scriptural Commands for Modern Times Living God's Word Today
Volume 2
Scriptural Commands for Modern Times Living God's Word
TodayVolume3

Introduction

As we embark on the journey through "Scriptural Commands for Modern Times- Living God's Word Today Volume 3," the third and final book in this series, it's important to recognize the significance of what lies ahead. This book represents the culmination of our exploration into how the timeless commands of the Bible can be applied to our modern lives. In a world that is constantly shifting, where values and beliefs seem to change with the wind, the Word of God remains a steadfast anchor. This final volume is designed to bring together all the lessons we've learned in the previous books, offering a comprehensive guide to living out God's commands in every area of our lives. Each chapter delves into specific teachings from Scripture, showing how they are not just ancient words but living truths that have the power to transform us today. Whether you're dealing with personal challenges, navigating relationships, or trying to find your purpose in a complex world, this book provides clear, practical guidance rooted in the unchanging truth of God's Word.

The commands of Scripture are more than just guidelines—they are a blueprint for a life that is fulfilling, purposeful, and aligned with God's will. As you read through these pages, you'll find that living according to God's commands brings peace in the midst of chaos, hope in times of despair, and direction when the path seems unclear. This final book in the series is an invitation to deepen your relationship with God by embracing His commands fully and allowing them to shape every aspect of your life. It's about understanding that these commands are not burdensome, but they are life-giving, offering us a way to navigate the complexities of the modern world with wisdom, grace, and confidence. As you turn each page, be prepared to be challenged, inspired, and equipped to live out your faith in a way that not only honors God but also impacts the world around you. "Scriptural Commands for Modern Times- Living God's Word Today Volume 3" is more than just a conclusion—it's the beginning of a new chapter in your spiritual journey, where the truths of Scripture become a living reality in your daily life. This book is here to help you carry forward the lessons of the entire series, applying them in a way that brings lasting change, deep fulfillment, and a closer walk with God. Let this final volume guide you as you continue to live out the powerful, transformative commands of God's Word, and watch how your life, and the lives of those around you, are changed for the better.

Chapter 1 – Disregard - "Do not fret because of evildoers"

Psalm 37:1 - "Fret not thyself because of evildoers, neither be thou envious against the workers of iniquity."

This verse emphasizes disregard, urging believers not to be anxious or envious of those who do wrong. To disregard the actions and apparent successes of evildoers means to trust in God's justice and focus on living righteously without being distracted or disturbed by the prosperity of the wicked. This disregard involves a steadfast dedication to trusting God's plan and timing, recognizing that His justice will ultimately prevail. This command encourages us to embrace a lifestyle of peace, contentment, and trust in God's sovereignty, rather than being consumed by worry or jealousy over the actions of others.

Disregarding evildoers begins with understanding that their apparent success is temporary and fleeting. The Bible consistently reminds us that the prosperity of the wicked is short-lived and that God's justice will ultimately be served. By keeping this perspective in mind, we can avoid becoming anxious or envious when we see evildoers thriving. This understanding helps us to maintain our focus on God and His promises, rather than being distracted by the temporary gains of those who do wrong. By trusting in God's justice, we can find peace and contentment in knowing that He is in control.

To disregard evildoers, we must cultivate a heart of trust in God. Trusting God means believing that He is in control and that His plans are for our good, even when circumstances seem unfair. By placing our trust in God's sovereignty, we can let go of our worries and anxieties about the actions of others. This trust helps us to remain focused on our own walk with God, rather than being consumed by what others are doing. As we trust in God's plan, we can experience the peace and security that come from knowing that He is working all things for our good.

Disregarding evildoers requires us to focus on our own actions and behavior. Instead of comparing ourselves to others or being envious of their success, we should strive to live according to God's principles and commands. By focusing on our own obedience and faithfulness, we can ensure that our lives are a reflection of God's love and righteousness. This focus helps to keep us grounded in our faith and prevents us from being swayed by the actions of others. As we concentrate on living righteously, we can demonstrate our commitment to God and His will.

To disregard evildoers, we must also cultivate a heart of contentment. Contentment means being satisfied with what God has provided and trusting that He knows what is best for us. By developing a content heart, we can avoid the trap of envy and jealousy. This contentment helps us to appreciate the blessings we have and to focus on the positive aspects of our lives. As we cultivate contentment, we can experience greater joy and peace, knowing that God is providing for our needs and guiding our path.

Disregarding evildoers involves being mindful of our thoughts and emotions. This means recognizing when we are starting to feel anxious or envious and taking steps to redirect our focus. By being aware of our internal state, we can prevent negative emotions from taking root and influencing our behavior. This mindfulness helps us to maintain a positive and trusting attitude, even in the face of challenges. As we practice being mindful of our thoughts and emotions, we can develop greater emotional resilience and stability.

To disregard evildoers, we must also be committed to prayer. Prayer is a powerful tool for seeking God's guidance, strength, and peace. By bringing our concerns and worries to God in prayer, we can find comfort and reassurance in His presence. Prayer helps us to connect with God and to receive the support we need to stay focused on Him. As we commit to regular prayer, we can strengthen our trust in God and our ability to disregard the actions of evildoers.

Disregarding evildoers requires us to be part of a supportive community of believers. Fellowship with other Christians provides encouragement, accountability, and support as we navigate the challenges of living righteously in a world where evildoers often seem to prosper. By sharing our experiences and struggles with others, we can receive the encouragement and strength we need to stay focused on God. This sense of community helps to reinforce our trust in God's justice and to remind us that we are not alone in our journey. Being part of a faith community provides a powerful source of encouragement and inspiration, helping us to stay committed to disregarding evildoers.

To disregard evildoers, we must also be committed to personal growth and spiritual development. This involves continually seeking to deepen our understanding of God's Word, to grow in our relationship with Him, and to develop our spiritual disciplines. By pursuing spiritual growth, we can strengthen our faith and our ability to trust in God's justice. This dedication to growth helps to ensure that our faith remains dynamic and alive, continually deepening our connection with God. As we grow spiritually, we can become more resilient in the face of challenges and better equipped to disregard the actions of evildoers.

Disregarding evildoers involves being mindful of our actions and their impact on others. This means considering how our behavior affects those around us and striving to be a positive influence. By acting with kindness, compassion, and integrity, we can reflect God's love and bring glory to Him. This mindfulness helps to create an environment where people feel valued and respected, and it demonstrates our dedication to living according to God's principles. As we seek to positively impact others, we can honor God through our relationships and interactions.

To disregard evildoers, we must also be willing to make sacrifices for the sake of our faith. This means being prepared to give up certain comforts, conveniences, or opportunities that conflict with our commitment to trusting in God's justice. Sacrifice is a key aspect of disregarding evildoers, as it demonstrates our willingness to prioritize

God's will above our own desires. By making sacrifices, we show that our faith is more important than worldly gain, and we strengthen our resolve to live according to God's principles. As we make sacrifices for our faith, we can live lives that honor and glorify God.

Disregarding evildoers requires us to be patient and persistent in our efforts. Living a life that honors God takes time and effort, and it requires us to remain steadfast in our commitment. By being patient and persistent, we can overcome the obstacles and distractions that seek to pull us away from our goal of disregarding evildoers. This perseverance helps to strengthen our faith and to deepen our dedication to God's will. As we remain patient and persistent in our pursuit of honoring God, we can live lives that are pleasing to Him.

To disregard evildoers, we must also be open to the guidance and direction of the Holy Spirit. The Holy Spirit provides the wisdom and strength we need to navigate life's challenges and to stay focused on our goal of disregarding evildoers. By being sensitive to the Spirit's leading, we can receive the support and encouragement needed to stay on the path of dedication to God's will. This openness to the Holy Spirit helps to ensure that our relationship with God is continually growing and deepening, allowing us to live lives that bring honor to Him.

Disregarding evildoers requires us to be grateful for the blessings and opportunities that God has given us. Gratitude helps us to maintain a positive and joyful attitude, even in the face of challenges and difficulties. By focusing on the goodness of God and expressing thankfulness, we can stay motivated and encouraged in our journey of faith. This gratitude helps to keep our hearts centered on God and to remind us of the importance of disregarding the actions of evildoers. As we cultivate a thankful heart, we can live lives that bring glory to God.

To disregard evildoers, we must also be willing to invest in the well-being of others. This means using our time, resources, and talents to serve and support those around us. By prioritizing the needs of others, we demonstrate the love of Jesus and fulfill His command to love our neighbor as ourselves. This commitment to serving others helps to cultivate a spirit of generosity and compassion, which are essential aspects of disregarding evildoers. As we invest in the well-being of others, we can live lives that bring honor and praise to God. Disregarding evildoers requires us to be honest and transparent in our relationships. This means being truthful in our words and actions and being willing to admit our mistakes and seek forgiveness. By practicing honesty, we build trust and credibility in our relationships, reflecting the integrity of Jesus. This commitment to truth helps to ensure that our interactions with others are genuine and authentic, allowing us to live lives that bring glory to God. As we embrace honesty, we can live lives that honor God with a sincere and truthful heart.

To disregard evildoers, we must also be willing to seek justice and to stand up for what is right. This means being willing to speak out against injustice and to take action to promote fairness and equality. By prioritizing justice, we demonstrate our commitment to living according to God's values and to making a positive impact in the world. This dedication to justice helps to ensure that our lives reflect the principles of God's kingdom, allowing us to live lives that bring glory to Him. Disregarding evildoers involves being mindful of our physical and emotional well-being. Taking care of our bodies and minds by getting enough rest, eating well, and seeking support when needed helps us to better manage the demands of following Jesus. By prioritizing self-care, we can ensure that we have the energy and resilience needed to continue our journey of disregarding evildoers. This mindfulness helps to sustain our commitment to following Jesus and to living a life that honors Him.

To disregard evildoers, we must also be willing to seek wisdom and guidance from others. This means being open to learning from the experiences and insights of mature believers. By seeking counsel and mentorship, we can gain valuable support and encouragement in our journey of disregarding evildoers. This openness to guidance helps to ensure that we are growing and maturing in our faith, allowing us to live lives that bring honor and praise to God. Disregarding evildoers requires a commitment to living out our faith in practical ways. This involves demonstrating our commitment to God through our actions, such as showing love, kindness, and compassion to others. By living out our faith, we can make a positive impact and provide a powerful witness to those around us. This practical expression of our faith helps to ensure that our lives reflect the principles of disregarding evildoers.

In conclusion, "Do not fret because of evildoers" is a powerful command that emphasizes disregard. Psalm 37:1 urges believers not to be anxious or envious of those who do wrong. Disregard involves understanding that the success of evildoers is temporary, cultivating trust in God, focusing on our own actions, developing contentment, being mindful of our thoughts and emotions, committing to prayer, being part of a supportive community, pursuing personal growth, being mindful of our impact on others, making sacrifices, being patient and persistent, seeking the Holy Spirit's guidance, expressing gratitude, investing in others, practicing honesty, seeking justice, prioritizing self-care, seeking wisdom, and living out our faith practically. By embracing this command, we can ensure that our lives reflect our commitment to disregarding evildoers and trusting in God's justice. In conclusion, "Do not fret because of evildoers" is a command that calls for disregard, encouraging us to trust in God's plan and to live righteously without being consumed by worry or envy over the actions of others.

Chapter 2 – Discretion - "Do not grieve the Holy Spirit"

Ephesians 4:30 - "And grieve not the holy Spirit of God, whereby ye are sealed unto the day of redemption."

This verse emphasizes discretion, urging believers to be mindful of their actions, words, and thoughts so that they do not cause sorrow or distress to the Holy Spirit. To grieve the Holy Spirit means to act in ways that are contrary to God's will and character, causing pain to the Spirit who dwells within us. This discretion involves a careful and thoughtful approach to living a life that honors God, consistently seeking to reflect His love, holiness, and truth. This command encourages us to embrace a lifestyle of sensitivity to the Spirit's leading, being aware of how our behavior impacts our relationship with God and our witness to others.

Discretion in not grieving the Holy Spirit begins with understanding the role of the Holy Spirit in our lives. The Holy Spirit is our Comforter, Guide, and Helper, who empowers us to live in a way that pleases God. The Spirit convicts us of sin, guides us into all truth, and helps us to grow in spiritual maturity. By recognizing the importance of the Holy Spirit, we can develop a deep respect and sensitivity to His presence in our lives. This understanding helps us to value the guidance and support of the Spirit, encouraging us to live in a way that honors Him.

To avoid grieving the Holy Spirit, we must cultivate a heart of obedience. Obedience means following God's commands and being responsive to the promptings of the Holy Spirit. By committing to obey God in every area of our lives, we demonstrate our dedication to His will and our desire to live according to His purposes. This obedience helps to ensure that our actions align with God's principles and that we are living in a way that pleases Him. As we cultivate a heart of obedience, we can experience the joy and peace that come from living in harmony with the Spirit.

Discretion in not grieving the Holy Spirit requires us to be mindful of our words. Our speech has the power to build up or tear down, to bless or to curse. By being careful with our words, we can avoid causing harm to others and grieving the Spirit. This mindfulness involves speaking with kindness, truth, and love, reflecting the character of Christ in our interactions. As we practice discretion in our speech, we can honor God and strengthen our relationships with others.

To avoid grieving the Holy Spirit, we must also be attentive to our thoughts. Our thoughts shape our attitudes and actions, and they can either align with God's will or lead us astray. By guarding our minds and focusing on what is true, noble, right, pure, lovely, and admirable, we can cultivate a mindset that honors God. This vigilance in our thought life helps us to remain sensitive to the Spirit's guidance and to live in a way that pleases God. As we fill our minds with godly thoughts, we can avoid grieving the Holy Spirit. Discretion in not grieving the Holy Spirit involves being mindful of our actions. Our behavior should reflect our commitment to Christ and our desire to live according to His teachings. By acting with integrity, compassion, and righteousness, we can honor God and avoid causing grief to the Spirit. This mindfulness helps to ensure that our actions are consistent with our faith and that we are living in a way that pleases God. As we practice discretion in our actions, we can strengthen our witness and bring glory to God.

To avoid grieving the Holy Spirit, we must also be willing to confess and repent of our sins. When we fall short and act in ways that displease God, it is important to acknowledge our wrongdoing and seek His forgiveness. By confessing our sins and turning away from them, we can restore our fellowship with God and receive His cleansing. This humility and willingness to repent help us to remain sensitive to the Spirit's conviction and to grow in spiritual maturity. As we practice confession and repentance, we can avoid grieving the Holy Spirit and experience the fullness of His grace.

Discretion in not grieving the Holy Spirit requires us to be part of a supportive community of believers. Fellowship with other Christians provides encouragement, accountability, and support as we seek to live lives that honor God. By sharing our experiences and challenges with others, we can receive the encouragement and strength we need to stay focused on God. This sense of community helps to reinforce our commitment to living according to God's will and to avoid grieving the Holy Spirit. Being part of a faith community provides a powerful source of encouragement and inspiration, helping us to stay committed to honoring the Spirit.

To avoid grieving the Holy Spirit, we must also be committed to personal growth and spiritual development. This involves continually seeking to deepen our understanding of God's Word, to grow in our relationship with Him, and to develop our spiritual disciplines. By pursuing spiritual growth, we can strengthen our commitment to living according to God's will and enhance our ability to reflect His character. This dedication to growth helps to ensure that our faith remains dynamic and alive, continually deepening our connection with God. As we grow spiritually, we can become more sensitive to the Spirit's leading and better equipped to avoid grieving Him.

Discretion in not grieving the Holy Spirit involves being mindful of our actions and their impact on others. This means considering how our behavior affects those around us and striving to be a positive influence. By acting with kindness, compassion, and integrity, we can reflect God's love and bring glory to Him. This mindfulness helps to create an environment where people feel valued and respected, and it demonstrates our dedication to living according to God's principles. As we seek to positively impact others, we can honor God through our relationships and interactions. To avoid grieving the Holy Spirit, we must also be willing to make sacrifices for the sake of our faith. This means being prepared to give up certain comforts, conveniences, or opportunities that conflict with our commitment to honoring God.

Sacrifice is a key aspect of living a life that pleases God and avoids grieving the Spirit. By making sacrifices, we show that our faith is more important than worldly gain, and we strengthen our resolve to live according to God's principles. As we make sacrifices for our faith, we can live lives that honor and glorify God.

Discretion in not grieving the Holy Spirit requires us to be patient and persistent in our efforts. Living a life that honors God takes time and effort, and it requires us to remain steadfast in our commitment. By being patient and persistent, we can overcome the obstacles and distractions that seek to pull us away from our goal of pleasing God. This perseverance helps to strengthen our faith and to deepen our dedication to God's will. As we remain patient and persistent in our pursuit of honoring God, we can live lives that are pleasing to Him.

To avoid grieving the Holy Spirit, we must also be open to the guidance and direction of the Holy Spirit. The Holy Spirit provides the wisdom and strength we need to navigate life's challenges and to stay focused on our goal of living according to God's will. By being sensitive to the Spirit's leading, we can receive the support and encouragement needed to stay on the path of dedication to God. This openness to the Holy Spirit helps to ensure that our relationship with God is continually growing and deepening, allowing us to live lives that bring honor to Him.

Discretion in not grieving the Holy Spirit requires us to be grateful for the blessings and opportunities that God has given us. Gratitude helps us to maintain a positive and joyful attitude, even in the face of challenges and difficulties. By focusing on the goodness of God and expressing thankfulness, we can stay motivated and encouraged in our journey of faith. This gratitude helps to keep our hearts centered on God and to remind us of the importance of honoring the Holy Spirit in everything we do. As we cultivate a thankful heart, we can live lives that bring glory to God.

To avoid grieving the Holy Spirit, we must also be willing to invest in the well-being of others. This means using our time, resources, and talents to serve and support those around us. By prioritizing the needs of others, we demonstrate the love of Jesus and fulfill His command to love our neighbor as ourselves. This commitment to serving others helps to cultivate a spirit of generosity and compassion, which are essential aspects of living according to God's will. As we invest in the well-being of others, we can live lives that bring honor and praise to God.

Discretion in not grieving the Holy Spirit requires us to be honest and transparent in our relationships. This means being truthful in our words and actions and being willing to admit our mistakes and seek forgiveness. By practicing honesty, we build trust and credibility in our relationships, reflecting the integrity of Jesus. This commitment to truth helps to ensure that our interactions with others are genuine and authentic, allowing us to live lives that bring glory to God. As we embrace honesty, we can live lives that honor God with a sincere and truthful heart.

To avoid grieving the Holy Spirit, we must also be willing to seek justice and to stand up for what is right. This means being willing to speak out against injustice and to take action to promote fairness and equality. By prioritizing justice, we demonstrate our commitment to living according to God's values and to making a positive impact in the world. This dedication to justice helps to ensure that our lives reflect the principles of God's kingdom, allowing us to live lives that bring glory to Him.

Discretion in not grieving the Holy Spirit involves being mindful of our physical and emotional well-being. Taking care of our bodies and minds by getting enough rest, eating well, and seeking support when needed helps us to better manage the demands of following Jesus. By prioritizing self-care, we can ensure that we have the energy and resilience needed to continue our journey of living according to God's will. This mindfulness helps to sustain our commitment to following Jesus and to living a life that honors Him.

To avoid grieving the Holy Spirit, we must also be willing to seek wisdom and guidance from others. This means being open to

learning from the experiences and insights of mature believers. By seeking counsel and mentorship, we can gain valuable support and encouragement in our journey of living according to God's will. This openness to guidance helps to ensure that we are growing and maturing in our faith, allowing us to live lives that bring honor and praise to God. Discretion in not grieving the Holy Spirit requires a commitment to living out our faith in practical ways. This involves demonstrating our commitment to God through our actions, such as showing love, kindness, and compassion to others. By living out our faith, we can make a positive impact and provide a powerful witness to those around us. This practical expression of our faith helps to ensure that our lives reflect the principles of discretion in not grieving the Holy Spirit.

In conclusion, "Do not grieve the Holy Spirit" is a powerful command that emphasizes discretion. Ephesians 4:30 urges believers to be mindful of their actions, words, and thoughts so that they do not cause sorrow or distress to the Holy Spirit. Discretion involves understanding the role of the Holy Spirit, cultivating a heart of obedience, being mindful of our words, thoughts, and actions, confessing and repenting of our sins, being part of a supportive community, committing to personal growth, being mindful of our impact on others, making sacrifices, being patient and persistent, seeking the Holy Spirit's guidance, expressing gratitude, investing in others, practicing honesty, seeking justice, prioritizing self-care, seeking wisdom, and living out our faith practically. By embracing this command, we can ensure that our lives reflect our commitment to not grieving the Holy Spirit and experiencing the fullness of His presence and guidance. In conclusion, "Do not grieve the Holy Spirit" is a command that calls for discretion, encouraging us to live in a way that honors God and reflects His love and holiness in everything we do.

"Do not grieve the Holy Spirit" is a command found in Ephesians 4:30, which says, "And grieve not the holy Spirit of God, whereby ye are sealed unto the day of redemption." This verse emphasizes discretion, urging believers to be mindful of their actions, words, and thoughts so that they do not cause sorrow or distress to the Holy Spirit. To grieve the Holy Spirit means to act in ways that are contrary to God's will and character, causing pain to the Spirit who dwells within us. This discretion involves a careful and thoughtful approach to living a life that honors God, consistently seeking to reflect His love, holiness, and truth. This command encourages us to embrace a lifestyle of sensitivity to the Spirit's leading, being aware of how our behavior impacts our relationship with God and our witness to others.

Discretion in not grieving the Holy Spirit begins with understanding the role of the Holy Spirit in our lives. The Holy Spirit is our Comforter, Guide, and Helper, who empowers us to live in a way that pleases God. The Spirit convicts us of sin, guides us into all truth, and helps us to grow in spiritual maturity. By recognizing the importance of the Holy Spirit, we can develop a deep respect and sensitivity to His presence in our lives. This understanding helps us to value the guidance and support of the Spirit, encouraging us to live in a way that honors Him.

To avoid grieving the Holy Spirit, we must cultivate a heart of obedience. Obedience means following God's commands and being responsive to the promptings of the Holy Spirit. By committing to obey God in every area of our lives, we demonstrate our dedication to His will and our desire to live according to His purposes. This obedience helps to ensure that our actions align with God's principles and that we are living in a way that pleases Him. As we cultivate a heart of obedience, we can experience the joy and peace that come from living in harmony with the Spirit.

Discretion in not grieving the Holy Spirit requires us to be mindful of our words. Our speech has the power to build up or tear down, to bless or to curse. By being careful with our words, we can avoid causing harm to others and grieving the Spirit. This mindfulness involves speaking with kindness, truth, and love, reflecting the character of Christ in our interactions. As we practice discretion in our speech, we can honor God and strengthen our relationships with others.

To avoid grieving the Holy Spirit, we must also be attentive to our thoughts. Our thoughts shape our attitudes and actions, and they can either align with God's will or lead us astray. By guarding our minds and focusing on what is true, noble, right, pure, lovely, and admirable, we can cultivate a mindset that honors God. This vigilance in our thought life helps us to remain sensitive to the Spirit's guidance and to live in a way that pleases God. As we fill our minds with godly thoughts, we can avoid grieving the Holy Spirit.

Discretion in not grieving the Holy Spirit involves being mindful of our actions. Our behavior should reflect our commitment to Christ and our desire to live according to His teachings. By acting with integrity, compassion, and righteousness, we can honor God and avoid causing grief to the Spirit. This mindfulness helps to ensure that our actions are consistent with our faith and that we are living in a way that pleases God. As we practice discretion in our actions, we can strengthen our witness and bring glory to God. To avoid grieving the Holy Spirit, we must also be willing to confess and repent of our sins. When we fall short and act in ways that displease God, it is important to acknowledge our wrongdoing and seek His forgiveness. By confessing our sins and turning away from them, we can restore our fellowship with God and receive His cleansing. This humility and willingness to repent help us to remain sensitive to the Spirit's conviction and to grow in spiritual maturity. As we practice confession and repentance, we can avoid grieving the Holy Spirit and experience the fullness of His grace.

Discretion in not grieving the Holy Spirit requires us to be part of a supportive community of believers. Fellowship with other Christians provides encouragement, accountability, and support as we seek to live lives that honor God. By sharing our experiences and challenges with others, we can receive the encouragement and strength we need to stay focused on God. This sense of community helps to reinforce our commitment to living according to God's will and to avoid grieving the Holy Spirit. Being part of a faith community provides a powerful source of encouragement and inspiration, helping us to stay committed to honoring the Spirit.

To avoid grieving the Holy Spirit, we must also be committed to personal growth and spiritual development. This involves continually seeking to deepen our understanding of God's Word, to grow in our relationship with Him, and to develop our spiritual disciplines. By pursuing spiritual growth, we can strengthen our commitment to living according to God's will and enhance our ability to reflect His character. This dedication to growth helps to ensure that our faith remains dynamic and alive, continually deepening our connection with God. As we grow spiritually, we can become more sensitive to the Spirit's leading and better equipped to avoid grieving Him.

Discretion in not grieving the Holy Spirit involves being mindful of our actions and their impact on others. This means considering how our behavior affects those around us and striving to be a positive influence. By acting with kindness, compassion, and integrity, we can reflect God's love and bring glory to Him. This mindfulness helps to create an environment where people feel valued and respected, and it demonstrates our dedication to living according to God's principles. As we seek to positively impact others, we can honor God through our relationships and interactions.

To avoid grieving the Holy Spirit, we must also be willing to make sacrifices for the sake of our faith. This means being prepared to give up certain comforts, conveniences, or opportunities that conflict with our commitment to honoring God. Sacrifice is a key aspect of living a life that pleases God and avoids grieving the Spirit. By making sacrifices, we show that our faith is more important than worldly gain, and we strengthen our resolve to live according to God's principles. As we make sacrifices for our faith, we can live lives that honor and glorify God.

Discretion in not grieving the Holy Spirit requires us to be patient and persistent in our efforts. Living a life that honors God takes time and effort, and it requires us to remain steadfast in our commitment. By being patient and persistent, we can overcome the obstacles and distractions that seek to pull us away from our goal of pleasing God. This perseverance helps to strengthen our faith and to deepen our dedication to God's will. As we remain patient and persistent in our pursuit of honoring God, we can live lives that are pleasing to Him.

To avoid grieving the Holy Spirit, we must also be open to the guidance and direction of the Holy Spirit. The Holy Spirit provides the wisdom and strength we need to navigate life's challenges and to stay focused on our goal of living according to God's will. By being sensitive to the Spirit's leading, we can receive the support and encouragement needed to stay on the path of dedication to God. This openness to the Holy Spirit helps to ensure that our relationship with God is continually growing and deepening, allowing us to live lives that bring honor to Him.

Discretion in not grieving the Holy Spirit requires us to be grateful for the blessings and opportunities that God has given us. Gratitude helps us to maintain a positive and joyful attitude, even in the face of challenges and difficulties. By focusing on the goodness of God and expressing thankfulness, we can stay motivated and encouraged in our journey of faith. This gratitude helps to keep our hearts centered on God and to remind us of the importance of honoring the Holy Spirit in everything we do. As we cultivate a thankful heart, we can live lives that bring glory to God.

To avoid grieving the Holy Spirit, we must also be willing to invest in the well-being of others. This means using our time, resources, and talents to serve and support those around us. By prioritizing the needs of others, we demonstrate the love of Jesus and fulfill His command to love our neighbor as ourselves. This commitment to serving others helps to cultivate a spirit of generosity and compassion, which are essential aspects of living according to God's will. As we invest in the well-being of others, we can live lives that bring honor and praise to God.

Discretion in not grieving the Holy Spirit requires us to be honest and transparent in our relationships. This means being truthful in our words and actions and being willing to admit our mistakes and seek forgiveness. By practicing honesty, we build trust and credibility in our relationships, reflecting the integrity of Jesus. This commitment to truth helps to ensure that our interactions with others are genuine and authentic, allowing us to live lives that bring glory to God. As we embrace honesty, we can live lives that honor God with a sincere and truthful heart.

To avoid grieving the Holy Spirit, we must also be willing to seek justice and to stand up for what is right. This means being willing to speak out against injustice and to take action to promote fairness and equality. By prioritizing justice, we demonstrate our commitment to living according to God's values and to making a positive impact in the world. This dedication to justice helps to ensure that our lives reflect the principles of God's kingdom, allowing us to live lives that bring glory to Him.

Discretion in not grieving the Holy Spirit involves being mindful of our physical and emotional well-being. Taking care of our bodies and minds by getting enough rest, eating well, and seeking support when needed helps us to better manage the demands of following Jesus. By prioritizing self-care, we can ensure that we have the energy and resilience needed to continue our journey of living according to God's will. This mindfulness helps to sustain our commitment to following Jesus and to living a life that honors Him.

To avoid grieving the Holy Spirit, we must also be willing to seek wisdom and guidance from others. This means being open to

learning from the experiences and insights of mature believers. By seeking counsel and mentorship, we can gain valuable support and encouragement in our journey of living according to God's will. This openness to guidance helps to ensure that we are growing and maturing in our faith, allowing us to live lives that bring honor and praise to God.

Discretion in not grieving the Holy Spirit requires a commitment to living out our faith in practical ways. This involves demonstrating our commitment to God through our actions, such as showing love, kindness, and compassion to others. By living out our faith, we can make a positive impact and provide a powerful witness to those around us. This practical expression of our faith helps to ensure that our lives reflect the principles of discretion in not grieving the Holy Spirit.

In conclusion, "Do not grieve the Holy Spirit" is a powerful command that emphasizes discretion. Ephesians 4:30 urges believers to be mindful of their actions, words, and thoughts so that they do not cause sorrow or distress to the Holy Spirit. Discretion involves understanding the role of the Holy Spirit, cultivating a heart of obedience, being mindful of our words, thoughts, and actions, confessing and repenting of our sins, being part of a supportive community, committing to personal growth, being mindful of our impact on others, making sacrifices, being patient and persistent, seeking the Holy Spirit's guidance, expressing gratitude, investing in others, practicing honesty, seeking justice, prioritizing self-care, seeking wisdom, and living out our faith practically. By embracing this command, we can ensure that our lives reflect our commitment to not grieving the Holy Spirit and experiencing the fullness of His presence and guidance. In conclusion, "Do not grieve the Holy Spirit" is a command that calls for discretion, encouraging us to live in a way that honors God and reflects His love and holiness in everything we do.

Chapter 5 – Disregard - "Do not love the world"

1 John 2:15 - "Love not the world, neither the things that are in the world. If any man love the world, the love of the Father is not in him."

This verse emphasizes disregard, urging believers not to be attached to the worldly values, desires, and possessions that can draw us away from God. To disregard the world means to prioritize our relationship with God above all else and to avoid being swayed by the temptations and distractions that the world offers. This disregard involves a steadfast dedication to living a life that is centered on God's love and purposes rather than on the fleeting and often superficial allure of worldly things. This command encourages us to embrace a lifestyle of spiritual focus, where our primary aim is to seek God's kingdom and righteousness.

Disregarding the world begins with understanding what "the world" refers to in this context. In the Bible, "the world" often represents the system of values and behaviors that are opposed to God's will. This includes materialism, selfish ambition, pride, and the pursuit of pleasure above all else. By recognizing the nature of the world's temptations, we can better understand why it is important to avoid loving the world. This understanding helps us to see the dangers of becoming too attached to things that can lead us away from God.

To disregard the world, we must cultivate a heart of contentment and gratitude. Contentment means being satisfied with what God has provided and trusting that He knows what is best for us. By developing a content heart, we can avoid the trap of constantly seeking more and more from the world. This contentment helps us to appreciate the blessings we have and to focus on the eternal riches that come from our relationship with God. As we cultivate gratitude, we can find joy and fulfillment in God's provision rather than in the temporary pleasures of the world.

Disregarding the world requires us to be intentional about our actions and decisions. This means making choices that reflect our commitment to God's values rather than being influenced by worldly desires. By being intentional, we can ensure that our lives are a reflection of God's love and righteousness. This intentionality helps to create a positive impact in our communities and to demonstrate our dedication to God's kingdom. As we make deliberate choices that align with God's will, we can live lives that bring honor and praise to Him.

To disregard the world, we must also be mindful of our thoughts and desires. Our thoughts shape our attitudes and actions, and they can either draw us closer to God or lead us away from Him. By guarding our minds and focusing on what is true, noble, right, pure, lovely, and admirable, we can cultivate a mindset that honors God. This vigilance in our thought life helps us to remain sensitive to the Spirit's guidance and to live in a way that pleases God. As we fill our minds with godly thoughts, we can avoid the influence of worldly temptations.

Disregarding the world involves being mindful of our actions and their impact on others. This means considering how our behavior affects those around us and striving to be a positive influence. By acting with kindness, compassion, and integrity, we can reflect God's love and bring glory to Him. This mindfulness helps to create an environment where people feel valued and respected, and it demonstrates our dedication to living according to God's principles. As we seek to positively impact others, we can honor God through our relationships and interactions.

To disregard the world, we must also be willing to make sacrifices for the sake of our faith. This means being prepared to give up certain comforts, conveniences, or opportunities that conflict with our commitment to following God's will. Sacrifice is a key aspect of disregarding the world, as it demonstrates our willingness to prioritize God's kingdom above our own desires. By making sacrifices, we show that our faith is more important than worldly gain, and we strengthen our resolve to live according to God's principles. As we make sacrifices for our faith, we can live lives that honor and glorify God.

Disregarding the world requires us to be part of a supportive community of believers. Fellowship with other Christians provides encouragement, accountability, and support as we navigate the challenges of living a life that is not conformed to worldly values. By sharing our experiences and struggles with others, we can receive the encouragement and strength we need to stay focused on God. This sense of community helps to reinforce our commitment to living according to God's will and to avoid being swayed by worldly temptations. Being part of a faith community provides a powerful source of encouragement and inspiration, helping us to stay committed to disregarding the world.

To disregard the world, we must also be committed to personal growth and spiritual development. This involves continually seeking to deepen our understanding of God's Word, to grow in our relationship with Him, and to develop our spiritual disciplines. By pursuing spiritual growth, we can strengthen our commitment to living according to God's will and enhance our ability to reflect His character. This dedication to growth helps to ensure that our faith remains dynamic and alive, continually deepening our connection with God. As we grow spiritually, we can become more resilient in the face of worldly temptations and better equipped to avoid loving the world.

Disregarding the world involves being mindful of our actions and their impact on others. This means considering how our behavior affects those around us and striving to be a positive influence. By acting with kindness, compassion, and integrity, we can reflect God's love and bring glory to Him. This mindfulness helps to create an environment where people feel valued and respected, and it demonstrates our dedication to living according to God's principles. As we seek to positively impact others, we can honor God through our relationships and interactions.

To disregard the world, we must also be willing to make sacrifices for the sake of our faith. This means being prepared to give up certain comforts, conveniences, or opportunities that conflict with our commitment to following God's will. Sacrifice is a key aspect of disregarding the world, as it demonstrates our willingness to prioritize God's kingdom above our own desires. By making sacrifices, we show that our faith is more important than worldly gain, and we strengthen our resolve to live according to God's principles. As we make sacrifices for our faith, we can live lives that honor and glorify God.

Disregarding the world requires us to be patient and persistent in our efforts. Living a life that honors God takes time and effort, and it requires us to remain steadfast in our commitment. By being patient and persistent, we can overcome the obstacles and distractions that seek to pull us away from our goal of disregarding the world. This perseverance helps to strengthen our faith and to deepen our dedication to God's will. As we remain patient and persistent in our pursuit of honoring God, we can live lives that are pleasing to Him.

To disregard the world, we must also be open to the guidance and direction of the Holy Spirit. The Holy Spirit provides the wisdom and strength we need to navigate life's challenges and to stay focused on our goal of living according to God's will. By being sensitive to the Spirit's leading, we can receive the support and encouragement needed to stay on the path of dedication to God's will. This openness to the Holy Spirit helps to ensure that our relationship with God is continually growing and deepening, allowing us to live lives that bring honor to Him.

Disregarding the world requires us to be grateful for the blessings and opportunities that God has given us. Gratitude helps us to maintain a positive and joyful attitude, even in the face of challenges and difficulties. By focusing on the goodness of God and expressing thankfulness, we can stay motivated and encouraged in our journey of faith. This gratitude helps to keep our hearts centered on God and to remind us of the importance of disregarding the world in everything we do. As we cultivate a thankful heart, we can live lives that bring glory to God.

To disregard the world, we must also be willing to invest in the well-being of others. This means using our time, resources, and talents to serve and support those around us. By prioritizing the needs of others, we demonstrate the love of Jesus and fulfill His command to love our neighbor as ourselves. This commitment to serving others helps to cultivate a spirit of generosity and compassion, which are essential aspects of disregarding the world. As we invest in the well-being of others, we can live lives that bring honor and praise to God.

Disregarding the world requires us to be honest and transparent in our relationships. This means being truthful in our words and actions and being willing to admit our mistakes and seek forgiveness. By practicing honesty, we build trust and credibility in our relationships, reflecting the integrity of Jesus. This commitment to truth helps to ensure that our interactions with others are genuine and authentic, allowing us to live lives that bring glory to God. As we embrace honesty, we can live lives that honor God with a sincere and truthful heart.

To disregard the world, we must also be willing to seek justice and to stand up for what is right. This means being willing to speak out against injustice and to take action to promote fairness and equality. By prioritizing justice, we demonstrate our commitment to living according to God's values and to making a positive impact in the world. This dedication to justice helps to ensure that our lives reflect the principles of God's kingdom, allowing us to live lives that bring glory to Him.

Disregarding the world involves being mindful of our physical and emotional well-being. Taking care of our bodies and minds by getting enough rest, eating well, and seeking support when needed helps us to better manage the demands of following Jesus. By prioritizing self-care, we can ensure that we have the energy and resilience needed to continue our journey of living according to God's will. This mindfulness helps to sustain our commitment to following Jesus and to living a life that honors Him.

To disregard the world, we must also be willing to seek wisdom and guidance from others. This means being open to learning from the experiences and insights of mature believers. By seeking counsel and mentorship, we can gain valuable support and encouragement in our journey of living

according to God's will. This openness to guidance helps to ensure that we are growing and maturing in our faith, allowing us to live lives that bring honor and praise to God.

Disregarding the world requires a commitment to living out our faith in practical ways. This involves demonstrating our commitment to God through our actions, such as showing love, kindness, and compassion to others. By living out our faith, we can make a positive impact and provide a powerful witness to those around us. This practical expression of our faith helps to ensure that our lives reflect the principles of disregarding the world.

In conclusion, "Do not love the world" is a powerful command that emphasizes disregard. 1 John 2:15 urges believers not to be attached to worldly values, desires, and possessions that can draw us away from God. Disregard involves understanding the nature of worldly temptations, cultivating contentment and gratitude, being intentional about our actions, guarding our thoughts and desires, being mindful of our impact on others, making sacrifices, being part of a supportive community, pursuing personal growth, being patient and persistent, seeking the Holy Spirit's guidance, expressing gratitude, investing in others, practicing honesty, seeking justice, prioritizing self-care, seeking wisdom, and living out our faith practically. By embracing this command, we can ensure that our lives reflect our commitment to disregarding the world and experiencing the fullness of God's love and presence. In conclusion, "Do not love the world" is a command that calls for disregard, encouraging us to prioritize our relationship with God above all else and to live lives that honor and glorify Him.

Chapter 6 – Displace - "Do not overcome with evil, but overcome evil with good"

Romans 12:21 - "Be not overcome of evil, but overcome evil with good."

This verse emphasizes the concept of displacement, urging believers to respond to evil not by reciprocating it but by displacing it with goodness. To displace evil with good means to act in ways that reflect God's love, kindness, and righteousness, even in the face of wrongdoing. This displacement involves a conscious and deliberate effort to let goodness prevail in our actions, thoughts, and responses. This command encourages us to adopt a lifestyle of positive action, where we actively seek to counteract negativity, harm, and injustice with love, compassion, and moral integrity.

Displacing evil with good begins with understanding the nature of evil and the transformative power of goodness. Evil can manifest in various forms, such as hatred, violence, injustice, and deceit. When we encounter evil, our natural reaction might be to retaliate or to harbor resentment. However, this command from Romans urges us to rise above such impulses and instead choose to respond with good. Goodness has the power to transform situations, heal wounds, and bring about positive change. By recognizing the strength and influence of good actions, we can commit to overcoming evil through positive means.

To displace evil with good, we must cultivate a heart of love and compassion. Love is the foundation of all good actions and is central to God's nature. By embracing love, we can respond to others with kindness and understanding, even when they wrong us. This love should extend to all people, regardless of how they treat us. Compassion allows us to see beyond someone's actions to their underlying needs and struggles. As we develop a compassionate heart, we can respond to evil with empathy and a desire to bring about healing and reconciliation. Displacing evil with good requires us to be intentional about our responses. When faced with evil, we must consciously choose to respond with actions that reflect

God's goodness. This might involve acts of kindness, forgiveness, patience, and generosity. By being intentional, we can break the cycle of negativity and create an environment where goodness prevails. This intentionality helps us to stay focused on God's principles and to ensure that our actions align with His will.

To displace evil with good, we must also be mindful of our thoughts and attitudes. Our thoughts influence our behavior and can either contribute to or counteract evil. By guarding our minds and focusing on positive, godly thoughts, we can cultivate an attitude that is resistant to evil. This mindfulness involves rejecting negative thoughts and replacing them with those that are true, noble, right, pure, lovely, and admirable. As we fill our minds with positive thoughts, we can better resist the temptation to respond to evil with more evil. Displacing evil with good involves being proactive in doing good. It is not enough to simply refrain from evil; we must actively seek opportunities to do good. This proactive approach can involve helping those in need, standing up for justice, showing kindness to strangers, and promoting peace in our communities. By taking the initiative to do good, we can create a ripple effect of positivity that can counteract the presence of evil. As we make a habit of doing good, we can demonstrate the transformative power of goodness.

To displace evil with good, we must also be willing to forgive. Forgiveness is a powerful tool for overcoming evil, as it releases us from the burden of resentment and allows us to move forward in peace. By forgiving those who have wronged us, we can break the cycle of hatred and retaliation. This forgiveness does not excuse the wrongdoing but instead reflects God's grace and mercy. As we practice forgiveness, we can experience healing and promote reconciliation.

Displacing evil with good requires us to be part of a supportive community of believers. Fellowship with other Christians provides encouragement, accountability, and support as we strive to respond to evil with good. By sharing our experiences and challenges with others, we can receive the strength and motivation needed to stay committed to this principle. This sense of community helps to reinforce our resolve and to remind us that we are not alone in our efforts. Being part of a faith community provides a powerful source of encouragement and inspiration, helping us to stay focused on displacing evil with good.

To displace evil with good, we must also be committed to personal growth and spiritual development. This involves continually seeking to deepen our understanding of God's Word, to grow in our relationship with Him, and to develop our spiritual disciplines. By pursuing spiritual growth, we can strengthen our ability to respond to evil with good and enhance our capacity to reflect God's character. This dedication to growth helps to ensure that our faith remains dynamic and alive, continually deepening our connection with God. As we grow spiritually, we can become more resilient in the face of evil and better equipped to overcome it with good.

Displacing evil with good involves being mindful of our actions and their impact on others. This means considering how our behavior affects those around us and striving to be a positive influence. By acting with kindness, compassion, and integrity, we can reflect God's love and bring glory to Him. This mindfulness helps to create an environment where people feel valued and respected, and it demonstrates our dedication to living according to God's principles. As we seek to positively impact others, we can honor God through our relationships and interactions.

To displace evil with good, we must also be willing to make sacrifices for the sake of our faith. This means being prepared to give up certain comforts, conveniences, or opportunities that conflict with our commitment to responding to evil with good. Sacrifice is a key aspect of displacing evil with good, as it demonstrates our willingness to prioritize God's will above our own desires. By making sacrifices, we show that our faith is more important than worldly gain, and we strengthen our resolve to live according to God's principles. As we make sacrifices for our faith, we can live lives that honor and glorify God.

Displacing evil with good requires us to be patient and persistent in our efforts. Overcoming evil with good takes time and effort, and it requires us to remain steadfast in our commitment. By being patient and persistent, we can overcome the obstacles and distractions that seek to pull us away from our goal of displacing evil with good. This perseverance helps to strengthen our faith and to deepen our dedication to God's will. As we remain patient and persistent in our pursuit of honoring God, we can live lives that are pleasing to Him.

To displace evil with good, we must also be open to the guidance and direction of the Holy Spirit. The Holy Spirit provides the wisdom and strength we need to navigate life's challenges and to stay focused on our goal of responding to evil with good. By being sensitive to the Spirit's leading, we can receive the support and encouragement needed to stay on the path of dedication to God's will. This openness to the Holy Spirit helps to ensure that our relationship with God is continually growing and deepening, allowing us to live lives that bring honor to Him.

Displacing evil with good requires us to be grateful for the blessings and opportunities that God has given us. Gratitude helps us to maintain a positive and joyful attitude, even in the face of challenges and difficulties. By focusing on the goodness of God and expressing thankfulness, we can stay motivated and encouraged in our journey of faith. This gratitude helps to keep our hearts centered on God and to remind us of the importance of responding to evil with good in everything we do. As we cultivate a thankful heart, we can live lives that bring glory to God.

To displace evil with good, we must also be willing to invest in the well-being of others. This means using our time, resources, and talents to serve and support those around us. By prioritizing the needs of others, we demonstrate the love of Jesus and fulfill His command to love our neighbor as ourselves. This commitment to serving others helps to cultivate a spirit of generosity and compassion, which are essential aspects of displacing evil with good. As we invest in the well-being of others, we can live lives that bring honor and praise to God.

Displacing evil with good requires us to be honest and transparent in our relationships. This means being truthful in our words and actions and being willing to admit our mistakes and seek forgiveness. By practicing honesty, we build trust and credibility in our relationships, reflecting the integrity of Jesus. This commitment to truth helps to ensure that our interactions with others are genuine and authentic, allowing us to live lives that bring glory to God. As we embrace honesty, we can live lives that honor God with a sincere and truthful heart.

To displace evil with good, we must also be willing to seek justice and to stand up for what is right. This means being willing to speak out against injustice and to take action to promote fairness and equality. By prioritizing justice, we demonstrate our commitment to living according to God's values and to making a positive impact in the world. This dedication to justice helps to ensure that our lives reflect the principles of God's kingdom, allowing us to live lives that bring glory to Him.

Displacing evil with good involves being mindful of our physical and emotional well-being. Taking care of our bodies and minds by getting enough rest, eating well, and seeking support when needed helps us to better manage the demands of following Jesus. By prioritizing self-care, we can ensure that we have the energy and resilience needed to continue our journey of responding to evil with good. This mindfulness helps to sustain our commitment to following Jesus and to living a life that honors Him.

To displace evil with good, we must also be willing to seek wisdom and guidance from others. This means being open to learning from the experiences and insights of mature believers. By seeking counsel and mentorship, we can gain valuable support and encouragement in our journey of living according to God's will. This openness to guidance helps to ensure that we are growing and maturing in our faith, allowing us to live lives that bring honor and praise to God.

Displacing evil with good requires a commitment to living out our faith in practical ways. This involves demonstrating our commitment to God through our actions, such as showing love, kindness, and compassion to others. By living out our faith, we can make a positive impact and provide a powerful witness to those around us. This practical expression of our faith helps to ensure that our lives reflect the principles of displacing evil with good.

In conclusion, "Do not be overcome with evil, but overcome evil with good" is a powerful command that emphasizes displacement. Romans 12:21 urges believers to respond to evil not by reciprocating it but by displacing it with goodness. Displacement involves understanding the nature of evil and the transformative power of goodness, cultivating a heart of love and compassion, being intentional about our responses, guarding our thoughts and attitudes, being proactive in doing good, practicing forgiveness, being part of a supportive community, pursuing personal growth, being mindful of our impact on others, making sacrifices, being patient and persistent, seeking the Holy Spirit's guidance, expressing gratitude, investing in others, practicing honesty, seeking justice, prioritizing self-care, seeking wisdom, and living out our faith practically. By embracing this command, we can ensure that our lives reflect our commitment to displacing evil with good and experiencing the fullness of God's love and presence. In conclusion, "Do not be overcome with evil, but overcome evil with good" is a command that calls for displacement, encouraging us to let goodness prevail in our actions, thoughts, and responses, and to live lives that honor and glorify God.

Chapter 7 – Disregard - "Do not repay evil for evil"

1 Peter 3:9 - "Not rendering evil for evil, or railing for railing: but contrariwise blessing; knowing that ye are thereunto called, that ye should inherit a blessing."

This verse emphasizes disregard, urging believers not to respond to evil actions with more evil, but instead to respond with blessings. To disregard the impulse to retaliate means to intentionally choose a higher path of love and kindness, even when wronged. This disregard involves a conscious and deliberate effort to break the cycle of negativity and to reflect the love and grace of God in our responses. This command encourages us to adopt a lifestyle of forgiveness, compassion, and positive action, where we actively seek to counteract negativity, harm, and injustice with goodness and blessing.

Disregarding the urge to repay evil with evil begins with understanding the nature of retaliation and its effects. Retaliation perpetuates a cycle of negativity, escalating conflicts and causing further harm. When we respond to evil with evil, we mirror the very behavior we oppose, allowing negativity to dominate our interactions. This approach goes against the teachings of Jesus, who called us to love our enemies and to pray for those who persecute us. By recognizing the destructive nature of retaliation, we can better understand the importance of breaking this cycle and choosing a different path.

To disregard the urge to retaliate, we must cultivate a heart of forgiveness and compassion. Forgiveness means letting go of the desire for revenge and releasing the hurt and anger caused by others' actions. Compassion allows us to see beyond someone's behavior to their underlying pain or struggles. By embracing forgiveness and compassion, we can respond to wrongdoing with understanding and kindness. This approach not only helps to heal our own hearts but also has the potential to transform the hearts of those who have wronged us. Disregarding the urge to repay evil with evil requires us to be intentional about our responses. When faced with harm or insult, we must consciously choose to respond with actions that reflect God's love and grace. This might involve offering a kind word, extending help, or simply refraining from retaliating. By being intentional, we can disrupt the cycle of negativity and create an environment where love and grace prevail. This intentionality helps us to stay focused on God's principles and to ensure that our actions align with His will.

To disregard the urge to retaliate, we must also be mindful of our thoughts and attitudes. Our thoughts shape our attitudes and actions, and they can either contribute to or counteract the urge to retaliate. By guarding our minds and focusing on positive, godly thoughts, we can cultivate an attitude that resists the temptation to respond to evil with more evil. This mindfulness involves rejecting negative thoughts and replacing them with those that are true, noble, right, pure, lovely, and admirable. As we fill our minds with positive thoughts, we can better resist the urge to retaliate and respond with blessings instead.

Disregarding the urge to repay evil with evil involves being proactive in doing good. It is not enough to simply refrain from retaliation; we must actively seek opportunities to do good, even to those who have wronged us. This proactive approach can involve acts of kindness, generosity, and support for others. By taking the initiative to do good, we can create a ripple effect of positivity that can counteract the presence of evil. As we make a habit of doing good, we can demonstrate the transformative power of kindness and grace.

To disregard the urge to retaliate, we must also be willing to bless those who harm us. Blessing others means wishing them well and praying for their well-being, even when they have caused us pain. This approach reflects the teachings of Jesus, who instructed us to love our enemies and to bless those who curse us. By blessing those who harm us, we can break the cycle of negativity and demonstrate the love of Christ. This act of blessing not only benefits the recipient but also helps to soften our own hearts and to foster a spirit of love and compassion.

Disregarding the urge to repay evil with evil requires us to be part of a supportive community of believers. Fellowship with other Christians provides encouragement, accountability, and support as we strive to respond to evil with good. By sharing our experiences and challenges with others, we can receive the strength and motivation needed to stay committed to this principle. This sense of community helps to reinforce our resolve and to remind us that we are not alone in our efforts. Being part of a faith community provides a powerful source of encouragement and inspiration, helping us to stay focused on disregarding the urge to retaliate.

To disregard the urge to retaliate, we must also be committed to personal growth and spiritual development. This involves continually seeking to deepen our understanding of God's Word, to grow in our relationship with Him, and to develop our spiritual disciplines. By pursuing spiritual growth, we can strengthen our ability to respond to evil with good and enhance our capacity to reflect God's character. This dedication to growth helps to ensure that our faith remains dynamic and alive, continually deepening our connection with God. As we grow spiritually, we can become more resilient in the face of wrongdoing and better equipped to respond with blessings.

Disregarding the urge to repay evil with evil involves being mindful of our actions and their impact on others. This means considering how our behavior affects those around us and striving to be a positive influence. By acting with kindness, compassion, and integrity, we can reflect God's love and bring glory to Him. This mindfulness helps to create an environment where people feel valued and respected, and it demonstrates our dedication to living according to God's principles. As we seek to positively impact others, we can honor God through our relationships and interactions.

To disregard the urge to retaliate, we must also be willing to make sacrifices for the sake of our faith. This means being prepared to give up certain comforts, conveniences, or opportunities that conflict with our commitment to responding to evil with good. Sacrifice is a key aspect of disregarding the urge to retaliate, as it demonstrates our willingness to prioritize God's will above our own desires. By making sacrifices, we show that our faith is more important than worldly gain, and we strengthen our resolve to live according to God's principles. As we make sacrifices for our faith, we can live lives that honor and glorify God.

Disregarding the urge to repay evil with evil requires us to be patient and persistent in our efforts. Overcoming the desire to retaliate takes time and effort, and it requires us to remain steadfast in our commitment. By being patient and persistent, we can overcome the obstacles and distractions that seek to pull us away from our goal of responding to evil with good. This perseverance helps to strengthen our faith and to deepen our dedication to God's will. As we remain patient and persistent in our pursuit of honoring God, we can live lives that are pleasing to Him.

To disregard the urge to retaliate, we must also be open to the guidance and direction of the Holy Spirit. The Holy Spirit provides the wisdom and strength we need to navigate life's challenges and to stay focused on our goal of responding to evil with good. By being sensitive to the Spirit's leading, we can receive the support and encouragement needed to stay on the path of dedication to God's will. This openness to the Holy Spirit helps to ensure that our relationship with God is continually growing and deepening, allowing us to live lives that bring honor to Him. Disregarding the urge to repay evil with evil requires us to be grateful for the blessings and opportunities that God has given us. Gratitude helps us to maintain a positive and joyful attitude, even in the face of challenges and difficulties. By focusing on the goodness of God and expressing thankfulness, we can stay motivated and encouraged in our journey of faith. This gratitude helps to keep our hearts centered on

God and to remind us of the importance of responding to evil with good in everything we do. As we cultivate a thankful heart, we can live lives that bring glory to God.

To disregard the urge to retaliate, we must also be willing to invest in the well-being of others. This means using our time, resources, and talents to serve and support those around us. By prioritizing the needs of others, we demonstrate the love of Jesus and fulfill His command to love our neighbor as ourselves. This commitment to serving others helps to cultivate a spirit of generosity and compassion, which are essential aspects of responding to evil with good. As we invest in the well-being of others, we can live lives that bring honor and praise to God. Disregarding the urge to repay evil with evil requires us to be honest and transparent in our relationships. This means being truthful in our words and actions and being willing to admit our mistakes and seek forgiveness. By practicing honesty, we build trust and credibility in our relationships, reflecting the integrity of Jesus. This commitment to truth helps to ensure that our interactions with others are genuine and authentic, allowing us to live lives that bring glory to God. As we embrace honesty, we can live lives that honor God with a sincere and truthful heart.

To disregard the urge to retaliate, we must also be willing to seek justice and to stand up for what is right. This means being willing to speak out against injustice and to take action to promote fairness and equality. By prioritizing justice, we demonstrate our commitment to living according to God's values and to making a positive impact in the world. This dedication to justice helps to ensure that our lives reflect the principles of God's kingdom, allowing us to live lives that bring glory to Him.

Disregarding the urge to repay evil with evil involves being mindful of our physical and emotional well-being. Taking care of our bodies and minds by getting enough rest, eating well, and seeking support when needed helps us to better manage the demands of following Jesus. By prioritizing self-care, we can ensure that we have the energy and resilience needed to continue our journey of responding to evil with good. This mindfulness helps to sustain our commitment to following Jesus and to living a life that honors Him.

To disregard the urge to

retaliate, we must also be willing to seek wisdom and guidance from others. This means being open to learning from the experiences and insights of mature believers. By seeking counsel and mentorship, we can gain valuable support and encouragement in our journey of living according to God's will. This openness to guidance helps to ensure that we are growing and maturing in our faith, allowing us to live lives that bring honor and praise to God.

Disregarding the urge to repay evil with evil requires a commitment to living out our faith in practical ways. This involves demonstrating our commitment to God through our actions, such as showing love, kindness, and compassion to others. By living out our faith, we can make a positive impact and provide a powerful witness to those around us. This practical expression of our faith helps to ensure that our lives reflect the principles of disregarding the urge to retaliate.

In conclusion, "Do not repay evil for evil" is a powerful command that emphasizes disregard. 1 Peter 3:9 urges believers not to respond to evil actions with more evil, but instead to respond with blessings. Disregard involves understanding the nature of retaliation and its effects, cultivating a heart of forgiveness and compassion, being intentional about our responses, guarding our thoughts and attitudes, being proactive in doing good, blessing those who harm us, being part of a supportive community, pursuing personal growth, being mindful of our impact on others, making sacrifices, being patient and persistent, seeking the Holy Spirit's guidance, expressing gratitude, investing in others, practicing honesty, seeking justice, prioritizing self-care, seeking wisdom, and living out our faith practically. By embracing this command, we can ensure that our lives reflect our commitment to disregarding the urge to retaliate and experiencing the fullness of God's love and presence.

In conclusion, "Do not repay evil for evil" is a command that calls for disregard, encouraging us to respond to wrongdoing with blessings and to live lives that honor and glorify God.

Chapter 8 - Distance "Do not be unequally yoked with unbelievers"

2 Corinthians 6:14 - "Be ye not unequally yoked together with unbelievers: for what fellowship hath righteousness with unrighteousness? and what communion hath light with darkness?" This verse emphasizes distance, urging believers to avoid forming close, binding relationships with those who do not share their faith in God. To distance oneself in this context means to maintain clear boundaries in relationships to ensure that one's faith and values are not compromised by close associations with those who do not follow Christ. This distance involves a careful and deliberate effort to protect one's spiritual integrity while still showing love and kindness to everyone. This command encourages us to adopt a lifestyle of discernment and intentionality, where we choose our closest relationships based on shared faith and values.

Distancing oneself from being unequally yoked begins with understanding the metaphor of the yoke. In biblical times, a yoke was a wooden beam used to pair two oxen together to work as a team in plowing fields. If the oxen were unequally yoked, meaning one was stronger or taller than the other, they would not be able to work effectively together. Similarly, in relationships, being unequally yoked with unbelievers can lead to conflicts, misunderstandings, and compromises that can hinder one's spiritual growth and commitment to God. By recognizing the importance of being equally yoked, we can understand why it is crucial to form close relationships with those who share our faith.

To avoid being unequally yoked, we must cultivate a heart of discernment. Discernment is the ability to judge well and to make wise choices based on God's Word and guidance. By developing discernment, we can evaluate potential relationships and determine whether they will support or hinder our spiritual journey. This discernment helps us to choose friendships, partnerships, and even romantic relationships that are aligned with our faith and values. As we practice discernment, we can build a support system that encourages us to grow closer to God.

Distancing oneself from being unequally yoked requires us to be intentional about our relationships. This means actively seeking out and nurturing connections with fellow believers who share our commitment to Christ. By prioritizing relationships with those who can provide spiritual encouragement, accountability, and support, we can strengthen our faith and avoid the pitfalls of being unequally yoked. This intentionality helps to create a community of believers who can walk alongside us in our faith journey, offering guidance and companionship.

To avoid being unequally yoked, we must also be mindful of our interactions with unbelievers. While it is important to love and reach out to those who do not share our faith, we must be cautious about forming deep, binding connections that could lead to compromise. This mindfulness involves setting healthy boundaries that allow us to maintain our spiritual integrity while still showing kindness and respect to others. By being mindful of our interactions, we can protect our faith and avoid situations that could lead to spiritual compromise.

Distancing oneself from being unequally yoked involves being proactive in building a strong foundation in faith. This means investing time in studying God's Word, praying, and growing in our relationship with Him. By strengthening our own faith, we can become more resilient to the influences of the world and more discerning in our relationships. This proactive approach helps to ensure that we are rooted in our faith and equipped to make wise choices in our interactions with others.

To avoid being unequally yoked, we must also be committed to personal growth and spiritual development. This involves continually seeking to deepen our understanding of God's Word, to grow in our relationship with Him, and to develop our spiritual disciplines. By pursuing spiritual growth, we can strengthen our commitment to living according to God's will and enhance our capacity to reflect His character. This dedication to growth helps to ensure that our faith remains dynamic and alive, continually deepening our connection with God. As we grow spiritually, we can become more resilient in the face of worldly influences and better equipped to avoid being unequally yoked.

Distancing oneself from being unequally yoked involves being mindful of our actions and their impact on others. This means considering how our behavior affects those around us and striving to be a positive influence. By acting with kindness, compassion, and integrity, we can reflect God's love and bring glory to Him. This mindfulness helps to create an environment where people feel valued and respected, and it demonstrates our dedication to living according to God's principles. As we seek to positively impact others, we can honor God through our relationships and interactions.

To avoid being unequally yoked, we must also be willing to make sacrifices for the sake of our faith. This means being prepared to give up certain relationships or opportunities that conflict with our commitment to following God's will. Sacrifice is a key aspect of avoiding being unequally yoked, as it demonstrates our willingness to prioritize God's kingdom above our own desires. By making sacrifices, we show that our faith is more important than worldly gain, and we strengthen our resolve to live according to God's principles. As we make sacrifices for our faith, we can live lives that honor and glorify God.

Distancing oneself from being unequally yoked requires us to be patient and persistent in our efforts. Building and maintaining relationships that are aligned with our faith takes time and effort, and it requires us to remain steadfast in our commitment. By being patient and persistent, we can overcome the obstacles and distractions that seek to pull us away from our goal of being equally yoked with fellow believers. This perseverance helps to strengthen our faith and to deepen our dedication to God's will. As we remain patient and persistent in our pursuit of honoring God, we can live lives that are pleasing to Him.

To avoid being unequally yoked, we must also be open to the guidance and direction of the Holy Spirit. The Holy Spirit provides the wisdom and strength we need to navigate life's challenges and to stay focused on our goal of living according to God's will. By being sensitive to the Spirit's leading, we can receive the support and encouragement needed to stay on the path of dedication to God's will. This openness to the Holy Spirit helps to ensure that our relationship with God is continually growing and deepening, allowing us to live lives that bring honor to Him. Distancing oneself from being unequally yoked requires us to be grateful for the blessings and opportunities that God has given us. Gratitude helps us to maintain a positive and joyful attitude, even in the face of challenges and difficulties. By focusing on the goodness of God and expressing thankfulness, we can stay motivated and encouraged in our journey of faith. This gratitude helps to keep our hearts centered on God and to remind us of the importance of forming relationships that are aligned with our faith. As we cultivate a thankful heart, we can live lives that bring glory to God.

To avoid being unequally yoked, we must also be willing to invest in the well-being of others. This means using our time, resources, and talents to serve and support those around us. By prioritizing the needs of others, we demonstrate the love of Jesus and fulfill His command to love our neighbor as ourselves. This commitment to serving others helps to cultivate a spirit of generosity and compassion, which are essential aspects of building relationships that honor God. As we invest in the well-being of others, we can live lives that bring honor and praise to God.

Distancing oneself from being unequally yoked requires us to be honest and transparent in our relationships. This means being truthful in our words and actions and being willing to admit our mistakes and seek forgiveness. By practicing honesty, we build trust and credibility in our relationships, reflecting the integrity of Jesus. This commitment to truth helps to ensure that our interactions with others are genuine and authentic, allowing us to live lives that bring glory to God. As we embrace honesty, we can live lives that honor God with a sincere and truthful heart.

To avoid being unequally yoked, we must also be willing to seek justice and to stand up for what is right. This means being willing to speak out against injustice and to take action to promote fairness and equality. By prioritizing justice, we demonstrate our commitment to living according to God's values and to making a positive impact in the world. This dedication to justice helps to ensure that our lives reflect the principles of God's kingdom, allowing us to live lives that bring glory to Him.

Distancing oneself from being unequally yoked involves being mindful of our physical and emotional well-being. Taking care of our bodies and minds by getting enough rest, eating well, and seeking support when needed helps us to better manage the demands of following Jesus. By prioritizing self-care, we can ensure that we have the energy and resilience needed to continue our journey of living according to God's will. This mindfulness helps to sustain our commitment to following Jesus and to living a life that honors Him.

To avoid being unequally yoked, we must also be willing to seek wisdom and guidance from others. This means being open to learning from the experiences and insights of mature believers. By seeking counsel and mentorship, we can gain valuable support and encouragement in our journey of living according to God's will. This openness to guidance helps to ensure that we are growing and maturing in our faith, allowing us to live lives that bring honor and praise to God.

Distancing oneself from being unequally yoked requires a commitment to living out our faith in practical ways. This involves demonstrating our commitment to God through our actions, such as showing love, kindness, and compassion to others. By living out our faith, we can make a positive impact and provide a powerful witness to those around us. This practical expression of our faith helps to ensure that our lives reflect the principles of avoiding being unequally yoked.

In conclusion, "Do not be unequally yoked with unbelievers" is a powerful command that emphasizes distance. 2 Corinthians 6:14 urges believers to avoid forming close, binding relationships with those who do not share their faith in God. Distance involves understanding the metaphor of the yoke, cultivating discernment, being intentional about our relationships, setting healthy boundaries, being proactive in building a strong foundation in faith, pursuing personal growth, being mindful of our actions, making sacrifices, being patient and persistent, seeking the Holy Spirit's guidance, expressing gratitude, investing in others, practicing honesty, seeking justice, prioritizing self-care, seeking wisdom, and living out our faith practically. By embracing this command, we can ensure that our lives reflect our commitment to maintaining spiritual integrity and experiencing the fullness of God's love and presence. In conclusion, "Do not be unequally yoked with unbelievers" is a command that calls for distance, encouraging us to form relationships that support and strengthen our faith while living lives that honor and glorify God.

Chapter 9 - Determination "Do not be weary in well doing"

Galatians 6:9 - "And let us not be weary in well doing: for in due season we shall reap, if we faint not."

This verse emphasizes distance, urging believers to avoid forming close, binding relationships with those who do not share their faith in God. To distance oneself in this context means to maintain clear boundaries in relationships to ensure that one's faith and values are not compromised by close associations with those who do not follow Christ. This distance involves a careful and deliberate effort to protect one's spiritual integrity while still showing love and kindness to everyone. This command encourages us to adopt a lifestyle of discernment and intentionality, where we choose our closest relationships based on shared faith and values.

Distancing oneself from being unequally yoked begins with understanding the metaphor of the yoke. In biblical times, a yoke was a wooden beam used to pair two oxen together to work as a team in plowing fields. If the oxen were unequally yoked, meaning one was stronger or taller than the other, they would not be able to work effectively together. Similarly, in relationships, being unequally yoked with unbelievers can lead to conflicts, misunderstandings, and compromises that can hinder one's spiritual growth and commitment to God. By recognizing the importance of being equally yoked, we can understand why it is crucial to form close relationships with those who share our faith.

To avoid being unequally yoked, we must cultivate a heart of discernment. Discernment is the ability to judge well and to make wise choices based on God's Word and guidance. By developing discernment, we can evaluate potential relationships and determine whether they will support or hinder our spiritual journey. This discernment helps us to choose friendships, partnerships, and even romantic relationships that are aligned with our faith and values. As we practice discernment, we can build a support system that encourages us to grow closer to God.

Distancing oneself from being unequally yoked requires us to be intentional about our relationships. This means actively seeking out and nurturing connections with fellow believers who share our commitment to Christ. By prioritizing relationships with those who can provide spiritual encouragement, accountability, and support, we can strengthen our faith and avoid the pitfalls of being unequally yoked. This intentionality helps to create a community of believers who can walk alongside us in our faith journey, offering guidance and companionship.

To avoid being unequally yoked, we must also be mindful of our interactions with unbelievers. While it is important to love and reach out to those who do not share our faith, we must be cautious about forming deep, binding connections that could lead to compromise. This mindfulness involves setting healthy boundaries that allow us to maintain our spiritual integrity while still showing kindness and respect to others. By being mindful of our interactions, we can protect our faith and avoid situations that could lead to spiritual compromise.

Distancing oneself from being unequally yoked involves being proactive in building a strong foundation in faith. This means investing time in studying God's Word, praying, and growing in our relationship with Him. By strengthening our own faith, we can become more resilient to the influences of the world and more discerning in our relationships. This proactive approach helps to ensure that we are rooted in our faith and equipped to make wise choices in our interactions with others.

To avoid being unequally yoked, we must also be committed to personal growth and spiritual development. This involves continually seeking to deepen our understanding of God's Word, to grow in our relationship with Him, and to develop our spiritual disciplines. By pursuing spiritual growth, we can strengthen our commitment to living according to God's will and enhance our capacity to reflect His character. This dedication to growth helps to ensure that our faith remains dynamic and alive, continually deepening our connection with God. As we grow spiritually, we can become more resilient in the face of worldly influences and better equipped to avoid being unequally yoked.

Distancing oneself from being unequally yoked involves being mindful of our actions and their impact on others. This means considering how our behavior affects those around us and striving to be a positive influence. By acting with kindness, compassion, and integrity, we can reflect God's love and bring glory to Him. This mindfulness helps to create an environment where people feel valued and respected, and it demonstrates our dedication to living according to God's principles. As we seek to positively impact others, we can honor God through our relationships and interactions.

To avoid being unequally yoked, we must also be willing to make sacrifices for the sake of our faith. This means being prepared to give up certain relationships or opportunities that conflict with our commitment to following God's will. Sacrifice is a key aspect of avoiding being unequally yoked, as it demonstrates our willingness to prioritize God's kingdom above our own desires. By making sacrifices, we show that our faith is more important than worldly gain, and we strengthen our resolve to live according to God's principles. As we make sacrifices for our faith, we can live lives that honor and glorify God.

Distancing oneself from being unequally yoked requires us to be patient and persistent in our efforts. Building and maintaining relationships that are aligned with our faith takes time and effort, and it requires us to remain steadfast in our commitment. By being patient and persistent, we can overcome the obstacles and distractions that seek to pull us away from our goal of being equally yoked with fellow believers. This perseverance helps to strengthen our faith and to deepen our dedication to God's will. As we remain patient and persistent in our pursuit of honoring God, we can live lives that are pleasing to Him.

To avoid being unequally yoked, we must also be open to the guidance and direction of the Holy Spirit. The Holy Spirit provides the wisdom and strength we need to navigate life's challenges and to stay focused on our goal of living according to God's will. By being sensitive to the Spirit's leading, we can receive the support and encouragement needed to stay on the path of dedication to God's will. This openness to the Holy Spirit helps to ensure that our relationship with God is continually growing and deepening, allowing us to live lives that bring honor to Him. Distancing oneself from being unequally yoked requires us to be grateful for the blessings and opportunities that God has given us. Gratitude helps us to maintain a positive and joyful attitude, even in the face of challenges and difficulties. By focusing on the goodness of God and expressing thankfulness, we can stay motivated and encouraged in our journey of faith. This gratitude helps to keep our hearts centered on God and to remind us of the importance of forming relationships that are aligned with our faith. As we cultivate a thankful heart, we can live lives that bring glory to God.

To avoid being unequally yoked, we must also be willing to invest in the well-being of others. This means using our time, resources, and talents to serve and support those around us. By prioritizing the needs of others, we demonstrate the love of Jesus and fulfill His command to love our neighbor as ourselves. This commitment to serving others helps to cultivate a spirit of generosity and compassion, which are essential aspects of building relationships that honor God. As we invest in the well-being of others, we can live lives that bring honor and praise to God.

Distancing oneself from being unequally yoked requires us to be honest and transparent in our relationships. This means being truthful in our words and actions and being willing to admit our mistakes and seek forgiveness. By practicing honesty, we build trust and credibility in our relationships, reflecting the integrity of Jesus. This commitment to truth helps to ensure that our interactions with others are genuine and authentic, allowing us to live lives that bring glory to God. As we embrace honesty, we can live lives that honor God with a sincere and truthful heart.

To avoid being unequally yoked, we must also be willing to seek justice and to stand up for what is right. This means being willing to speak out against injustice and to take action to promote fairness and equality. By prioritizing justice, we demonstrate our commitment to living according to God's values and to making a positive impact in the world. This dedication to justice helps to ensure that our lives reflect the principles of God's kingdom, allowing us to live lives that bring glory to Him.

Distancing oneself from being unequally yoked involves being mindful of our physical and emotional well-being. Taking care of our bodies and minds by getting enough rest, eating well, and seeking support when needed helps us to better manage the demands of following Jesus. By prioritizing self-care, we can ensure that we have the energy and resilience needed to continue our journey of living according to God's will. This mindfulness helps to sustain our commitment to following Jesus and to living a life that honors Him.

To avoid being unequally yoked, we must also be willing to seek wisdom and guidance from others. This means being open to learning from the experiences and insights of mature believers. By seeking counsel and mentorship, we can gain valuable support and encouragement in our journey of living according to God's will. This openness to guidance helps to ensure that we are growing and maturing in our faith, allowing us to live lives that bring honor and praise to God.

Distancing oneself from being unequally yoked requires a commitment to living out our faith in practical ways. This involves demonstrating our commitment to God through our actions, such as showing love, kindness, and compassion to others. By living out our faith, we can make a positive impact and provide a powerful witness to those around us. This practical expression of our faith helps to ensure that our lives reflect the principles of avoiding being unequally yoked.

In conclusion, "Do not be unequally yoked with unbelievers" is a powerful command that emphasizes distance. 2 Corinthians 6:14 urges believers to avoid forming close, binding relationships with those who do not share their faith in God. Distance involves understanding the metaphor of the yoke, cultivating discernment, being intentional about our relationships, setting healthy boundaries, being proactive in building a strong foundation in faith, pursuing personal growth, being mindful of our actions, making sacrifices, being patient and persistent, seeking the Holy Spirit's guidance, expressing gratitude, investing in others, practicing honesty, seeking justice, prioritizing self-care, seeking wisdom, and living out our faith practically. By embracing this command, we can ensure that our lives reflect our commitment to maintaining spiritual integrity and experiencing the fullness of God's love and presence. In conclusion, "Do not be unequally yoked with unbelievers" is a command that calls for distance, encouraging us to form relationships that support and strengthen our faith while living lives that honor and glorify God.

Chapter 10 – Defend - "Defend the cause of the weak"

Psalm 82:3 - "Defend the poor and fatherless: do justice to the afflicted and needy."

This verse emphasizes the importance of defending those who are vulnerable and unable to defend themselves. To defend the cause of the weak means to stand up for the rights of the poor, the fatherless, the afflicted, and the needy, ensuring that they receive justice and protection. This defense involves a commitment to using our voice, resources, and actions to support those who are marginalized and oppressed. This command encourages us to adopt a lifestyle of advocacy, compassion, and active involvement in the pursuit of justice for all individuals, regardless of their circumstances.

Defending the cause of the weak begins with understanding the nature of vulnerability and the challenges faced by those who are poor, fatherless, afflicted, and needy. These individuals often lack the resources, support, and opportunities necessary to thrive and are frequently subjected to injustice and neglect. By recognizing their struggles, we can develop a deep sense of empathy and a strong desire to advocate for their rights and well-being. This understanding helps us to see the importance of taking action to support and defend those who are vulnerable.

To defend the cause of the weak, we must cultivate a heart of compassion and empathy. Compassion involves feeling genuine concern for the suffering of others and a desire to alleviate their pain. Empathy allows us to put ourselves in their shoes and understand their experiences and emotions. By developing compassion and empathy, we can be more motivated to take action on behalf of the weak and to advocate for their rights. This compassionate approach helps us to connect with those in need and to provide meaningful support and assistance. Defending the cause of the weak requires us to be intentional about our actions and advocacy. This means actively seeking out opportunities to support and defend those who are vulnerable, whether through volunteering, donating resources, or participating in advocacy efforts. By being intentional, we can ensure that our efforts are focused and effective in making a positive impact. This intentionality helps to create a culture of justice and compassion, where the needs of the weak are prioritized and addressed.

To defend the cause of the weak, we must also be willing to speak out against injustice and to use our voice to advocate for change. This involves raising awareness about the issues faced by the vulnerable and calling for action to address these challenges. By speaking out, we can influence public opinion, mobilize support, and encourage policymakers to implement changes that benefit the weak. This advocacy is essential for creating a society where justice and fairness prevail and where the rights of all individuals are protected. Defending the cause of the weak involves being proactive in providing support and assistance. This means offering practical help to those in need, such as providing food, shelter, healthcare, and education. By meeting their immediate needs, we can help to improve their quality of life and provide a foundation for long-term stability and success. This proactive approach demonstrates our commitment to justice and compassion and helps to create a more equitable and supportive society.

To defend the cause of the weak, we must also be committed to personal growth and development. This involves continually seeking to deepen our understanding of social justice issues and to develop our skills and knowledge in advocacy and support. By pursuing personal growth, we can become more effective advocates and defenders of the weak, and we can better understand the complexities of the issues they face. This dedication to growth helps to ensure that our efforts are informed and impactful, allowing us to make a meaningful difference in the lives of those we support. Defending the cause of the weak requires us to be part of a supportive community of like-minded individuals. Fellowship with others who share our commitment to justice and compassion provides encouragement, accountability, and support as we work to defend the vulnerable. By collaborating with others, we can amplify our efforts and create a stronger and more cohesive advocacy movement. This sense of community helps to reinforce our resolve and to remind us that we are not alone in our efforts. Being part of a supportive community provides a powerful source of encouragement and inspiration, helping us to stay committed to defending the cause of the weak.

To defend the cause of the weak, we must also be willing to make sacrifices for the sake of justice. This means being prepared to give up certain comforts, conveniences, or opportunities in order to support those who are vulnerable. Sacrifice is a key aspect of defending the cause of the weak, as it demonstrates our willingness to prioritize their needs above our own desires. By making sacrifices, we show that our commitment to justice is more important than personal gain, and we strengthen our resolve to live according to God's principles. As we make sacrifices for justice, we can live lives that honor and glorify God.

Defending the cause of the weak requires us to be patient and persistent in our efforts. Achieving justice and support for the vulnerable takes time and effort, and it requires us to remain steadfast in our commitment. By being patient and persistent, we can overcome the obstacles and challenges that seek to hinder our advocacy efforts. This perseverance helps to strengthen our faith and to deepen our dedication to God's will. As we remain patient and persistent in our pursuit of justice, we can live lives that are pleasing to Him.

To defend the cause of the weak, we must also be open to the guidance and direction of the Holy Spirit. The Holy Spirit provides the wisdom and strength we need to navigate the challenges of advocacy and to stay focused on our goal of supporting the vulnerable. By being sensitive to the Spirit's leading, we can receive the support and encouragement needed to stay on the path of dedication to God's will. This openness to the Holy Spirit helps to ensure that our relationship with God is continually growing and deepening, allowing us to live lives that bring honor to Him.

Defending the cause of the weak requires us to be grateful for the blessings and opportunities that God has given us. Gratitude helps us to maintain a positive and joyful attitude, even in the face of challenges and difficulties. By focusing on the goodness of God and expressing thankfulness, we can stay motivated and encouraged in our journey of faith. This gratitude helps to keep our hearts centered on God and to remind us of the importance of advocating for those who are vulnerable. As we cultivate a thankful heart, we can live lives that bring glory to God. To defend the cause of the weak, we must also be willing to invest in the well-being of others. This means using our time, resources, and talents to serve and support those around us. By prioritizing the needs of others, we demonstrate the love of Jesus and fulfill His command to love our neighbor as ourselves. This commitment to serving others helps to cultivate a spirit of generosity and compassion, which are essential aspects of defending the cause of the weak. As we invest in the well-being of others, we can live lives that bring honor and praise to God.

Defending the cause of the weak requires us to be honest and transparent in our advocacy efforts. This means being truthful in our words and actions and being willing to admit our mistakes and seek forgiveness. By practicing honesty, we build trust and credibility in our advocacy work, reflecting the integrity of Jesus. This commitment to truth helps to ensure that our interactions with others are genuine and authentic, allowing us to live lives that bring glory to God. As we embrace honesty, we can live lives that honor God with a sincere and truthful heart. To defend the cause of the weak, we must also be willing to seek justice and to stand up for what is right. This means being willing to speak out against injustice and to take action to promote fairness and equality. By prioritizing justice, we demonstrate our commitment to living according to God's values and to making a positive impact in the world. This dedication to justice helps to ensure that our lives reflect the principles of God's kingdom, allowing us to live lives that bring glory to Him.

Defending the cause of the weak involves being mindful of our physical and emotional well-being. Taking care of our bodies and minds by getting enough rest, eating well, and seeking support when needed helps us to better manage the demands of advocacy work. By prioritizing self-care, we can ensure that we have the energy and resilience needed to continue our journey of defending the vulnerable. This mindfulness helps to sustain our commitment to following Jesus and to living a life that honors Him. To defend the cause of the weak, we must also be willing to seek wisdom and guidance from others. This means being open to learning from the experiences and insights of mature believers and experienced advocates. By seeking counsel and mentorship, we can gain valuable support and encouragement in our journey of living according to God's will. This openness to guidance helps to ensure that we are growing and maturing in our faith, allowing us to live lives that bring honor and praise to God.

Defending the cause of the weak requires a commitment to living out our faith in practical ways. This involves demonstrating our commitment to God through our actions, such as showing love, kindness, and compassion to others. By living out our faith, we can make a positive impact and provide a powerful witness to those around us. This practical expression of our faith helps to ensure that our lives reflect the principles of defending the cause of the weak.

In conclusion, "Defend the cause of the weak" is a powerful command that emphasizes defense. Psalm 82:3 urges believers to stand up for the rights of the poor, the fatherless, the afflicted, and the needy, ensuring that they receive justice and protection. Defense involves understanding the nature of vulnerability, cultivating compassion and empathy, being intentional about our actions and advocacy, speaking out against injustice, providing practical support, pursuing personal growth, being part of a supportive community, making sacrifices, being patient and persistent, seeking the Holy Spirit's guidance, expressing gratitude, investing in others, practicing honesty, seeking justice, prioritizing self-care, seeking wisdom, and living out our faith practically. By embracing this command, we can ensure that our lives reflect our commitment to defending the cause of the weak and experiencing the fullness of God's love and presence. In conclusion, "Defend the cause of the weak" is a command that calls for defense, encouraging us to advocate for justice and support for those who are vulnerable, while living lives that honor and glorify God.

Conclusion

As we reach the conclusion of "Scriptural Commands for Modern Times- Living God's Word Today Volume 3," the final book in this series, it's a moment to reflect on the journey we've taken together. This book, like the ones before it, has been about more than just understanding the commands of Scripture—it's been about learning how to live them out in our everyday lives, no matter how challenging or complicated the world around us may be. We've explored how these ancient truths remain relevant today, offering us clear guidance, hope, and direction in a world that often feels overwhelming. Throughout this series, we've seen that God's commands are not restrictive rules meant to limit our freedom but are instead pathways to a life filled with peace, purpose, and joy. As you close this final volume, it's important to remember that the journey doesn't end here. The truths you've discovered and the lessons you've learned are meant to be carried forward into every day of your life. Living out God's Word is a continuous process, one that requires daily commitment and a heart open to His leading. The commands we've studied are not just for the pages of this book; they are for the moments when life gets tough, when decisions are hard, and when you're searching for the right path. By applying these commands, you can live a life that not only honors God but also brings light and hope to those around you. This final book is an invitation to take what you've learned and make it a living part of who you are, shaping your thoughts, actions, and relationships. As you go forward, let these commands be your guide, your comfort, and your strength. Remember that God's Word is not just a relic of the past but a living, breathing source of wisdom that speaks directly to your life today. The journey through this series may be ending, but the real adventure of living out these commands is just beginning. Let the teachings of this book inspire you to live boldly, love deeply, and walk faithfully in the path that God has set before you. As you continue to grow in your faith and apply these truths, may you find that they lead you to a life that is rich with meaning, filled with God's love, and anchored in His unchanging truth. The impact of living out these commands will not only transform your life but will also ripple out to touch the lives of others, bringing them closer to the God who loves them and desires the best for them. So, as you close this final chapter, take with you the knowledge that God's commands are not just rules to follow but are the keys to a life well-lived, a life that reflects His love and truth in every moment.

Don't miss out!

Visit the website below and you can sign up to receive emails whenever Joshua Rhoades publishes a new book. There's no charge and no obligation.

https://books2read.com/r/B-A-AJLBB-IGAZE

BOOKS 2 READ

Connecting independent readers to independent writers.

Did you love *Scriptural Commands for Modern Times Living God's Word TodayVolume3*? Then you should read *Scriptural Commands for Modern Times Living God's Word Today Volume 2*[1] by Joshua Rhoades!

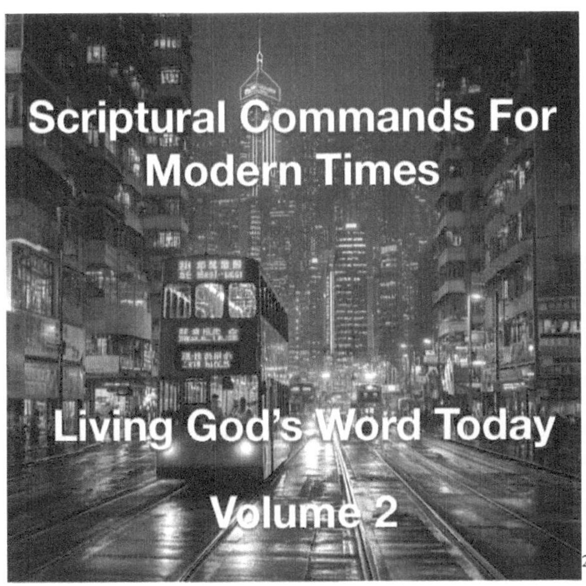

In today's world, where uncertainty and confusion seem to be the norm, the Bible offers a steady source of guidance and truth that is just as relevant now as it was thousands of years ago. "Scriptural Commands for Modern Times- Living God's Word Today Volume 2" continues the journey we began in the first volume, diving deeper into the commands of Scripture that are designed to help us navigate the complexities of life. This book is here to show that the Bible's teachings are not just old words on a page but living instructions that can help us face the challenges of today with wisdom and confidence. Throughout these pages, you'll find practical insights on how to apply God's commands to real-life situations, whether you're dealing with relationships, making tough

---

1. https://books2read.com/u/bzyP29

2. https://books2read.com/u/bzyP29

decisions, or trying to live with integrity in a world that often seems to reward the opposite. Each chapter is a reminder that God's Word is not just about what we should avoid but about the kind of life we are called to live—a life full of purpose, peace, and the deep satisfaction that comes from following God's path. As you read through this book, you'll discover how these ancient commands speak directly to the issues we face in our modern lives, offering clear and practical guidance for how to live in a way that honors God and brings out the best in us. The commands we explore are not just rules to follow but are invitations to experience life the way God intended—full of love, joy, and meaning. By the end of this volume, you'll see how these commands can shape your thoughts, guide your actions, and influence every part of your life, helping you to grow closer to God and become the person He created you to be. So, as you turn these pages, be ready to be challenged, inspired, and equipped to live out God's Word in a world that needs His truth more than ever. This book is not just a continuation but a deeper dive into the life-changing power of Scripture, and it's an invitation to let God's commands transform your life from the inside out.